917.3
NAU

Nault, Jennifer
American States Fact Book

AMERICAN STATES
FACT BOOK

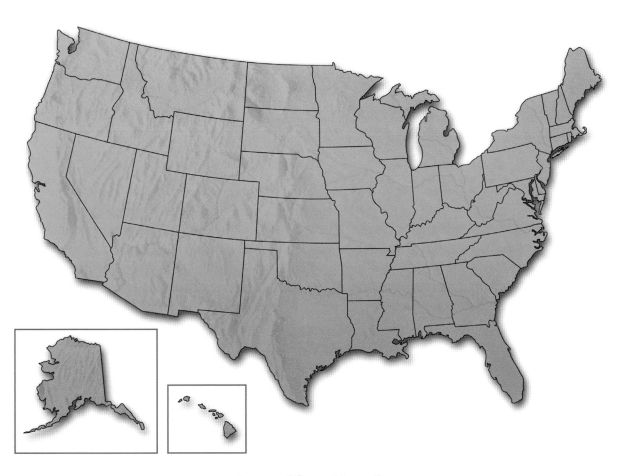

Jennifer Nault

Published by Weigl Publishers Inc.
123 South Broad Street, Box 227
Mankato, MN 56002
USA
Web site: www.weigl.com
Copyright © 2003 WEIGL PUBLISHERS INC.

Library of Congress Cataloging-in-Publication Data available upon request from the publisher. Fax: (507) 388-2746 for the attention of the Publishing Records Department.

ISBN 1-59036-031-1

Printed in the United States of America
1 2 3 4 5 6 7 8 9 10   06 05 04 03 02

Project Coordinator
Jennifer Nault
Copy Editor
Tina Schwartzenberger
Design and Layout
Terry Paulhus
Bryan Pezzi
Photo Researcher
Tina Schwartzenberger

Photograph Credits
Every reasonable effort has been made to trace ownership and to obtain permission to reprint copyright material. The publishers would be pleased to have any errors or omissions brought to their attention so that they may be corrected in subsequent printings.

Cover: Statue of Liberty (Corel) U.S. Flag (EyeWire/gettyimages); **Jim Argo:** page 24B; **Arizona Office of Tourism/Chris Coe:** page 24T; **Bob & Suzanne Clemenz:** page 22B; **Comstock, Inc.:** page 20B; **Corbis Corporation:** pages 3T, 6B, 8B, 12T, 12B, 16T, 16B; **Corel Corporation:** pages 3B, 4BR, 6T, 7B, 10T, 13, 14T, 14B, 17B, 20T; **Kevin Fleming/CORBIS/MAGMA:** page 22T; **Houghton/Mifflin Company:** page 26B; **Jessen Associates Inc./R. Silberlatt:** page 11BL; **Bruce Leighty:** page 9T; **Map Resources:** pages 5T, 5M, 5R, 7TL, 7TR, 7ML, 7MR, 11T; **Clark James Mishler:** page 11BR; **Oklahoma Tourism/Fred W. Marvel:** page 3M; **Terry Paulhus:** pages 7B, 9B, 17T, 27; **PhotoSpin, Inc.:** pages 4T, 4BL, 19, 29; **Michael C. Snell/Shade of the Cottonwood, L.L.C.:** page 8T; **South Dakota Tourism/Chad Copess:** page 18B; **Courtesy of United States Geological Survey, data from Landsat 7:** page 10B; **Visit Florida:** page 18T; **Washington State Historical Society:** pages 26T (PORT LEW 2), 28 (CURTIS 11635); **U.S. Census Bureau:** pages 21T, 23T, 23B, 25.

CONTENTS

INTRODUCTION

The United States of America covers the middle section of the continent of North America. It stretches across North America, from the Atlantic Ocean in the east to the Pacific Ocean in the west.

The United States is a federal republic, consisting of fifty states and the District of Columbia. Alaska and Hawai'i are the only non-contiguous, or non-touching, states in the nation. In 1776, the British colonies in North America declared independence. During the following two centuries, the original thirteen states were joined by thirty-seven new states. Today, the United States of America is the third-largest country in the world in population. In terms of land area, it is the fourth-largest country in the world.

The United States is a country where people from many nations and ethnic backgrounds have come together and formed a common identity. While U.S. citizens share many cultural similarities, their varied ethnic backgrounds make for different traditions, customs, and languages.

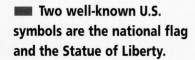

■ Two well-known U.S. symbols are the national flag and the Statue of Liberty.

■ Each year, about 4 million visitors explore the wonders of the Grand Canyon.

GEOGRAPHY

Rocky Mountains

The United States is located between Canada and Mexico, on the continent of North America. Alaska occupies the extreme northwestern region of North America, while Hawai'i is a group of islands located in the middle of the Pacific Ocean. The United States is bordered by Canada for 5,526 miles and by Mexico for 2,067 miles. Excluding Alaska and Hawai'i, the United States is often divided into seven major regions. Each region shares similarities in geography, climate, and economy. The regions are: New England, the Middle Atlantic States, the Southern States, the Midwestern States, the Rocky Mountain States, the Southwestern States, and the Pacific Coast States.

Ten Largest States by Total Area

	State	Size (sq. miles)
1	Alaska	615,230
2	Texas	267,277
3	California	158,869
4	Montana	147,046
5	New Mexico	121,598
6	Arizona	114,006
7	Nevada	110,567
8	Colorado	104,100
9	Wyoming	97,808
10	Oregon	97,132

Source: U.S. Census Bureau Statistical Abstract, 2000

Ten Smallest States by Total Area

	State	Size (sq. miles)
1	Rhode Island	1,231
2	Delaware	2,396
3	Connecticut	5,544
4	Hawai'i	6,459
5	New Jersey	8,215
6	Massachusetts	9,241
7	New Hampshire	9,283
8	Vermont	9,615
9	Maryland	12,297
10	West Virginia	24,231

Source: U.S. Census Bureau Statistical Abstract, 2000

The Midwest has fertile soil that is well suited for agriculture.

Source: Map Resources

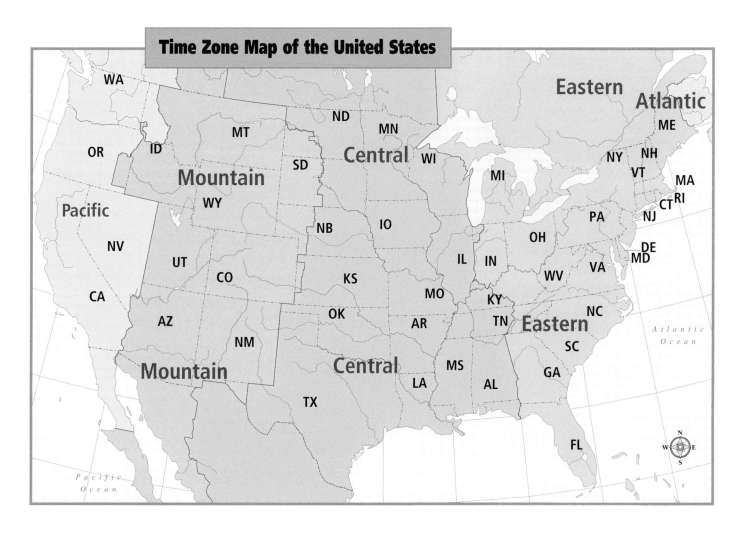

Time Zone Map of the United States

WA

OR

ID

MT

ND

MN

Central

Mountain

SD

WI

MI

Eastern

Atlantic

ME

NY

NH

VT

MA

Pacific

WY

NB

IO

OH

PA

CT RI

NJ

NV

UT

CO

KS

IL

IN

WV

VA

DE

MD

CA

MO

KY

AZ

OK

AR

TN

Eastern

NC

NM

Mountain

Central

MS

AL

GA

SC

Atlantic
Ocean

LA

TX

FL

Pacific
Ocean

▨▨ The craggy and mountainous terrain of the Hawai'ian Islands
makes for spectacular waterfalls, such as the Rainbow Falls in Hilo.

Top Ten States with the Longest Shorelines

	State	Miles of Shoreline
1	Alaska	33,904
2	Florida	8,426
3	Louisiana	7,721
4	Maine	3,478
5	California	3,427
6	North Carolina	3,375
7	Texas	3,359
8	Virginia	3,315
9	Maryland	3,190
10	Washington	3,026

Source: Map Resources

GETTING AROUND

There are many modes of transport available within the United States. Travelers and cargo can move from place to place via automobile, train, airplane, and ferry, to name a few. Ships and airplanes transport most international travelers and cargo to and from the U.S. The nation's first railroad line was built in Massachusetts in 1826. Before long, the network of railroads spread across the continent. Today, there are 140,275 miles of mainline railroad routes. For residents traveling via highway, there are approximately 3.56 million miles of paved roads. For water travelers, there are 25,482 miles of navigable inland waterways, excluding the Great Lakes. For those preferring air travel, there are 14,720 airports in the country.

A large network of rivers in the United States provides transportation routes for bulk cargo.

Top Ten States with Most National Highways

	State	Highways (miles)
1	Texas	13,435
2	California	7,622
3	Illinois	5,688
4	Pennsylvania	5,446
5	New York	5,140
6	Michigan	4,721
7	Georgia	4,596
8	Florida	4,358
9	Ohio	4,345
10	Wisconsin	4,172

Source: U.S. Department of Transportation FHWA, 2000

Top Ten Water Ports Ranked by Total Trade Tons

	Location	Tons (millions)
1	South Louisiana, LA	218
2	Houston, TX	191
3	New York, NY and NJ	139
4	New Orleans, LA	91
5	Corpus Christi, TX	83
=	Beaumont, TX	83
7	Huntington, WV	77
8	Long Beach, CA	70
9	Baton Rouge, LA	66
10	Texas City, TX	62

Source: U.S. Army Corps of Engineers, 2000

Chicago's O'Hare International Airport is one of the busiest airports in the United States.

Top Ten Airports in the U.S. with Most Boarded Passengers

	Airport	Million Passengers/Year
1	William B. Hartsfield Intl., Atlanta, GA	37.2
2	O'Hare Intl., Chicago, IL	31.5
3	Dallas/Fort Worth, Intl., Dallas/Fort Worth, TX	27.6
4	Los Angeles, Intl., Los Angeles, CA	24.0
5	Denver Intl., Denver, CO	17.4
6	Wayne County, Detroit, MI	16.6
7	San Francisco Intl., San Francisco, CA	16.4
8	Phoenix Sky Harbor Intl., Phoenix, AZ	16.1
9	Minneapolis Intl., Minneapolis, MN	15.4
10	McCarren Intl., Las Vegas, NV	15.3

Source: U.S. Department of Transportation, 1999

Top Ten Airports in the U.S. with Most Boarded Passengers

LAND

The United States covers an area of 3.62 million square miles. The terrain in the northern United States was formed by large ice sheets that covered much of North America until about 10,000 years ago. The land of the United States is as varied as it is vast. It ranges from Alaska's permafrost and rugged terrain to the prairies of the Midwest that stretch out for miles. The snow-capped Rocky Mountains lie in the west, and hilly terrain is found in the east. Warm beaches are found in the south, and in the southwest, desert prevails.

The land is rich in natural resources. Major deposits of valuable minerals, such as petroleum, lie underground. Much of the land is fertile and is used for farming.

Highest Peak Elevations in the United States

	Mountain/State	Height (ft.)
1	Mt. McKinley, AK	20,320
2	Mt. Whitney, CA	14,494
3	Mt. Elbert, CO	14,433
4	Mt. Ranier, WA	14,411
5	Gannett Peak, WY	13,804
6	Mauna Kea, HI	13,796
7	Kings Peak, UT	13,528
8	Wheeler Peak, NM	13,161
9	Boundary Peak, NV	13,143
10	Borah Peak, ID	12,662

Source: www.americasroof.com

Ten Largest Freshwater Lakes in the United States*

	Lake/State	Size (sq. miles)
1	Lake Michigan, IL, IN, MI, WI	22,400
2	Lake Iliamna, AK	1,000
3	Lake Okeechobee, FL	700
4	Becharof Lake, AK	458
5	Red Lake, MN	451
6	Teshekpuk Lake, AK	315
7	Naknek Lake, AK	242
8	Lake Winnebago, WI	215
9	Mille Lacs Lake, MN	207
10	Flathead Lake, MT	197

Source: Bartleby Encyclopedia

*Excluding lakes that are partly in Canada

Satellite Image of Vegetation Cover

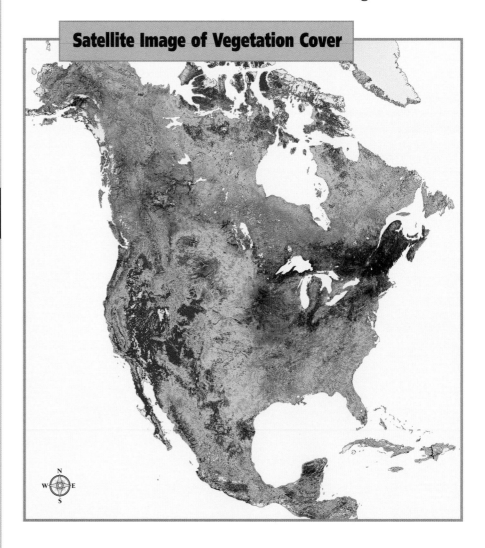

Topographical Map of the United States

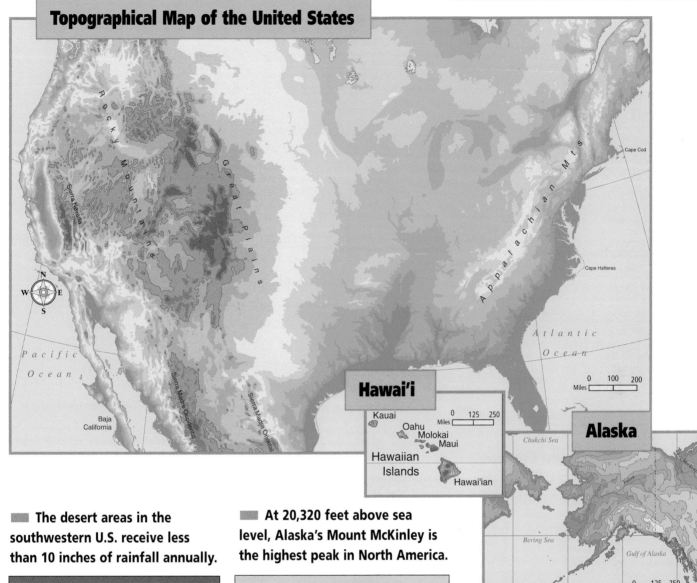

N
W E
S

Rocky Mountains

Sierra Nevada

Great Plains

Appalachian Mts

Cape Cod

Cape Hatteras

Atlantic
Ocean

Pacific
Ocean

Baja
California

Sierra Madre Occidental

Sierra Madre Oriental

0 100 200
Miles

Hawai'i

Kauai
Oahu
Molokai
Maui
Hawaiian
Islands
Hawai'ian

0 125 250
Miles

Alaska

Chukchi Sea

Bering Sea

Gulf of Alaska

0 125 250
Miles

The desert areas in the southwestern U.S. receive less than 10 inches of rainfall annually.

At 20,320 feet above sea level, Alaska's Mount McKinley is the highest peak in North America.

Ten Longest Rivers in the United States

	River	Length (miles)
1	Missouri River	2,540
2	Mississippi River	2,340
3	Yukon River	1,980
4	St. Lawrence River	1,900
=	Rio Grande	1,900
6	Arkansas River	1,460
7	Colorado River	1,450
8	Atchafalaya River	1,420
9	Ohio River	1,310
10	Red River	1,290

Source: U.S. Geological Survey

CLIMATE

Most parts of the United States experience seasonal changes in temperature. Precipitation is moderate in most areas, although coastal regions tend to receive greater amounts of rainfall. New England and the Midwest experience warm summers and cold winters. Areas near the Pacific Ocean, along with locations near large bodies of water, have milder temperatures throughout the year. In the West, mountainous areas are cool and receive more precipitation than the plains and plateaus in the Midwest. Small areas of the West and Southwest have an arid, desert climate. Summers are hotter and winters are milder in the South.

The Midwest and Southwest Regions of the country are prone to tornadoes. Other natural hazards include hurricanes, which occur primarily along the Atlantic Ocean and the Gulf of Mexico coasts.

▬▬ **The northeast and upper Midwest of the United States receive large amounts of snow in the winter.**

▬▬ **Cumulonimbus clouds are known as thunderheads. These clouds usually bring heavy rainfall and thunderstorms.**

Top Ten States with Greatest Percentage of Possible Sunshine

	State	Sunshine (%)
1	El Paso, TX	80
2	Albuquerque, NM	76
3	Honolulu, HI	74
4	Los Angeles, CA	72
5	Reno, NV	69
6	Denver, CO	67
7	Cheyenne, WY	64
=	New York, NY	64
=	Oklahoma City, OK	64
10	Wichita, KS	62

Source: U.S. Census Bureau Statistical Abstract, 2000

Top Ten States with Record High Temperatures

135
130
125
120
115
110
105
°F 100

Lake Havasu City, AZ, June 29, 1994
Ozark, AR, August 10, 1936
Greenland Ranch, CA, July 10, 1913
Alton, (near) KS, July 24, 1936
Laughlin, NV, June 29, 1994
Waste Isolat Pilot Plt, NM, June 27, 1994
Steele, ND, July 6, 1936
Tipton, OK, June 27, 1994
Pendleton, OR, August 10, 1898
Gannvalley, SD, July 5, 1936

Top Ten States with Record Low Temperatures

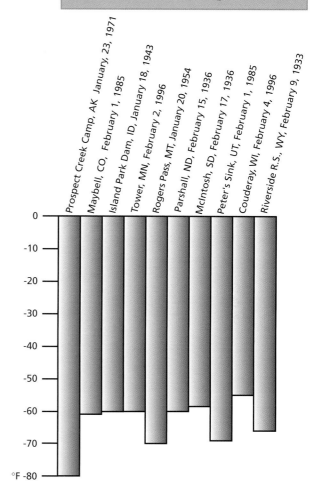

Prospect Creek Camp, AK January 23, 1971
Maybell, CO, February 1, 1985
Island Park Dam, ID, January 18, 1943
Tower, MN, February 2, 1996
Rogers Pass, MT, January 20, 1954
Parshall, ND, February 15, 1936
McIntosh, SD, February 17, 1936
Peter's Sink, UT, February 1, 1985
Couderay, WI, February 4, 1996
Riverside R.S., WY, February 9, 1933

0
-10
-20
-30
-40
-50
-60
-70
°F -80

Desert plants, such as cacti, store water in their thick leaves. These plants are found in the arid Southwest of the United States.

Cities with Most Annual Precipitation in the U.S.	
State	**Inches**
1 Mobile, AL	64
2 New Orleans, LA	62
3 Miami, FL	56
4 Jackson, MS	55
5 Juneau, AK	54
6 Memphis, TN	52
7 Atlanta, GA	51
= Little Rock, AK	51
9 Columbia, SC	50
10 New York, NY	47

Source: U.S. Census Bureau Statistical Abstract, 2000

■ **The Indian paintbrush is a common U.S. wildflower.**

Most Common Trees in the United States

1	Silver maple
2	Black cherry
3	Box elder
4	Eastern cottonwood
5	Black willow
6	Northern red oak
7	Flowering dogwood
8	Black oak
9	Ponderosa pine
10	Coast douglas fir

Source: American Forests

Most Common Birds in the United States

1	Red-winged blackbird
2	European starling
3	American robin
4	Mourning dove
5	Common grackle
6	American crow
7	Western meadowlark
8	House sparrow
9	Northern cardinal
10	Cliff sparrow

Source: U.S. Fish and Wildlife Service

PLANTS AND ANIMALS

From grizzly bears to Gila monsters to sea turtles, there is a large diversity of wildlife in the United States. The country has many animal refuge areas aimed at protecting wildlife. For instance, Yellowstone National Park, America's first national park, encompasses 2.2 million square acres.

The plant varieties in the United States are just as diverse as the wildlife. Plants range from desert cacti to California redwoods, the largest trees in the world. Although the United States was once almost entirely covered by trees and grasslands, human development has turned large areas into farmland and urban areas.

■ **The bald eagle has been the national symbol of the United States since 1782. This bird appears on the $1 bill.**

American State Symbols

State	Animal	Bird	Flower
Alabama	n/a	yellowhammer	camellia
Alaska	moose	willow ptarmigan	forget-me-not
Arizona	ringtail	cactus wren	saguaro cactus blossom
Arkansas	white-tailed deer	mockingbird	apple blossom
California	California grizzly bear	California quail	poppy
Colorado	bighorn sheep	lark bunting	Rocky Mt. columbine
Connecticut	sperm whale	robin	mountain laurel
Delaware	n/a	blue hen chicken	peach blossom
Florida	Florida panther	mockingbird	orange blossom
Georgia	right whale	brown thrasher	Cherokee rose
Hawai'i	humpback whale	nene	hibiscus
Idaho	n/a	mountain bluebird	syringa
Illinois	white-tailed deer	cardinal	purple violet
Indiana	n/a	cardinal	peony
Iowa	n/a	eastern goldfinch	wild prairie rose
Kansas	bison	western meadowlark	sunflower
Kentucky	gray squirrel	cardinal	goldenrod
Louisiana	Louisiana black bear	eastern brown pelican	magnolia
Maine	moose	chickadee	white pine cone
Maryland	n/a	Baltimore oriole	black-eyed Susan
Massachusetts	n/a	chickadee	mayflower
Michigan	white-tailed deer	robin	apple blossom
Minnesota	n/a	common loon	lady's slipper
Mississippi	white-tailed deer	mockingbird	magnolia
Missouri	Missouri mule	bluebird	hawthorn
Montana	grizzly bear	western meadowlark	bitterroot
Nebraska	white-tailed deer	western meadowlark	goldenrod
Nevada	desert bighorn sheep	mountain bluebird	sagebrush
New Hampshire	white-tailed deer	purple finch	purple lilac
New Jersey	horse	eastern goldfinch	violet
New Mexico	black bear	roadrunner	yucca flower
New York	beaver	bluebird	rose
North Carolina	gray squirrel	cardinal	dogwood
North Dakota	n/a	western meadowlark	wild prairie rose
Ohio	white-tailed deer	cardinal	scarlet carnation
Oklahoma	buffalo	scissor-tailed flycatcher	mistletoe
Oregon	American beaver	western meadowlark	Oregon grape
Pennsylvania	white-tailed deer	ruffed grouse	mountain laurel
Rhode Island	n/a	Rhode Island red hen	violet
South Carolina	white-tailed deer	Great Carolina wren	yellow jessamine
South Dakota	coyote	ring-necked pheasant	pasque
Tennessee	raccoon	mockingbird	iris
Texas	Texas longhorn/armadillo	mockingbird	bluebonnet
Utah	Rocky Mountain elk	California seagull	sego lily
Vermont	Morgan horse	hermit thrush	red clover
Virginia	n/a	cardinal	dogwood
Washington	n/a	goldfinch	pink rhododendron
West Virginia	black bear	cardinal	rhododendron
Wisconsin	badger	robin	wood violet
Wyoming	bison	western meadowlark	Indian paintbrush

INDUSTRY

The United States has the largest economy in the world. The country is also the most powerful in technology industries. Private individuals and businesses dominate the country's market-oriented economy. Business firms in the United States are global leaders in technology, such as computer software. The United States also leads the world in the production of high-technology medical, aerospace, and military equipment.

▬ **The United States is the largest agricultural exporter in the world.**

Top Ten Corporations in the United States*

	Corporation	Revenue/Year
1	General Motors	$177 billion
2	Wal-Mart	$165 billion
3	Ford Motor Co.	$163 billion
4	Exxon Mobil	$161 billion
5	General Electric	$112 billion
6	IBM	$86 billion
7	Citigroup	$82 billion
8	AT&T	$62 billion
=	Philip Morris	$62 billion
10	Boeing	$58 billion

Source: Forbes

*Based on the most recent year of earnings

▬ **Manufacturing industries, such as the production of automobiles, employ about 17 percent of the American population.**

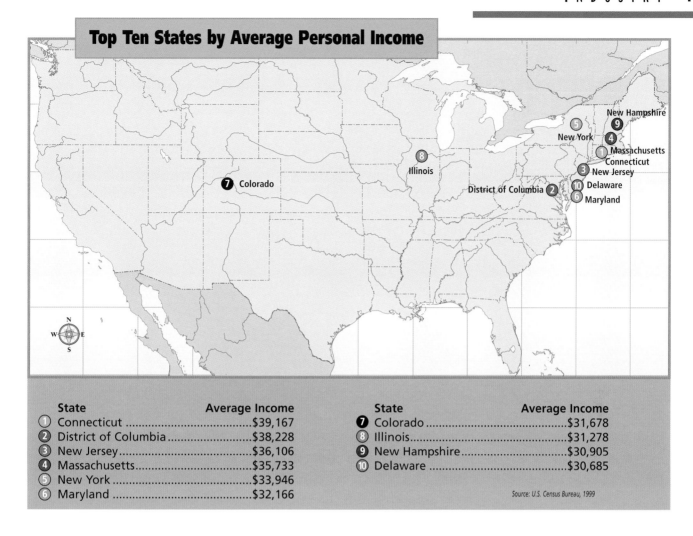

Top Ten States by Average Personal Income

State	Average Income
① Connecticut	$39,167
② District of Columbia	$38,228
③ New Jersey	$36,106
④ Massachusetts	$35,733
⑤ New York	$33,946
⑥ Maryland	$32,166

State	Average Income
❼ Colorado	$31,678
⑧ Illinois	$31,278
⑨ New Hampshire	$30,905
⑩ Delaware	$30,685

Source: U.S. Census Bureau, 1999

■■■ The yearly value of commercial fish and shellfish in the United States is about $3.5 million.

Top Ten Goods Exported from the United States (by value)

1	Electrical machinery
2	Automatic data processing equipment
3	Airplanes
4	General industrial machinery
5	Power-generating machinery
6	Specialized industrial machinery
7	Scientific instruments
8	Televisions and VCRs
9	Chemicals
10	Airplane parts

Source: U.S. Census Bureau, 1999

TOURISM

People from all over the world flock to the United States to explore its fascinating sights. In addition, the United States is so vast and varied that many tourists are U.S. residents, traveling from other parts of the country.

Some of the main attractions in the United States include festivals, such as the annual celebration of Mardi Gras in New Orleans, Louisiana, and theme parks, such as Disneyland in California. With its many neon lights, Las Vegas, Nevada is a hot tourist destination. National parks, such as the Grand Canyon National Park, are also large tourist draws. Large cities, such as Chicago, New York, and San Francisco, offer world-class entertainment and restaurants to travelers. Hawai'i is a tropical paradise for vacationers wishing to relax and enjoy the surf and sun.

Most Visited Amusement and Theme Parks

Park	Yearly Visitors (millions)
1	The Magic Kingdom	15.2
2	Disneyland	13.5
3	Epcot Center	10.1
4	Disney-MGM Studios	8.7
5	Disney's Animal Kingdom	8.6
6	Universal Studios Florida	8.1
7	Universal Studios Hollywood	5.1
8	Sea World Florida	4.7
9	Busch Gardens	3.9
10	Six Flags Great Adventure	3.8

Source: The Top 10 of Everything 2001, published by Dorling Kindersley

Top Ten States Visited by People from Overseas

State	Yearly Visitors (millions)
1	Florida	6.1
2	California	6.0
3	New York	5.3
4	Hawai'i	2.8
5	Nevada	1.9
6	Illinois	1.3
7	Massachusetts	1.2
8	Texas	1.1
9	Arizona	0.85
=	New Jersey	0.85

Source: U.S. Department of Commerce, International Trade Administration

■■■■ The 60-foot busts of George Washington, Thomas Jefferson, Theodore Roosevelt, and Abraham Lincoln carved into Mount Rushmore are a popular tourist attraction. Visitors to the area can also see sculptor Gutzon Borglum's studio.

Top Ten Most Visited National Parks in the U.S.

National Park	Number of Visitors (millions)
1. Great Smoky Mountains (NC/TN) This national park is heavily forested; the area is known for its Southern Appalachian Mountain culture.	10.0
2. Grand Canyon (AZ) The deep-walled Grand Canyon is 277 miles long, up to 18 miles wide, and more than 5,000 feet deep.	4.2
3. Yosemite (CA) Along with its many groves of giant sequoia trees, this park is known for its high cliffs and waterfalls.	3.7
4. Olympic (WA) Eight kinds of plants and five kinds of animals that are found in Olympic National Park are found nowhere else in the world.	3.6
5. Yellowstone (MT/ID/WY) Established on March 1, 1872, Yellowstone National Park is the oldest national park in the world. The Old Faithful Geyser, and about 10,000 other hot springs and geysers, are found in the park.	3.1
6. Rocky Mountain (CO) This park contains peaks that tower more than 13,000 feet. At 14,255 feet, Longs Peak is the highest peak in the park.	3.0
7. Grand Teton (WY) The Teton Range is the youngest range of mountains in the Rockies.	2.8
8. Acadia (ME) Acadia is the first national park to be established east of the Mississippi River. It is believed that Native Americans lived in the area more than 5,000 years ago.	2.6
9. Zion (UT) Zion National Park is the site of the world's largest arch, the Kolob Arch. Its span measures 310 feet.	2.4
10. Mammoth Cave (KY) Mammoth Cave contains the largest recorded cave system in the world, with more than 336 miles of mapped caves.	2.1

Las Vegas, Nevada is a center for tourism and conventions. The tourism industry is the city's largest employer.

Top Ten International Airports for Passengers Traveling to the U.S.

	Airport	Yearly Travelers (millions)
1	London Heathrow, U.K.	10.7
2	Tokyo Narita, Japan	9.8
3	Toronto Lester B. Pearson, Canada	8.4
4	Frankfurt, Germany	6.1
=	Paris Charles de Gaulle, France	6.1
6	London Gatwick, U.K.	5.7
7	Amsterdam Schiphol, the Netherlands	4.7
8	Mexico City, Mexico	4.5
9	Vancouver, Canada	3.9
10	Osaka Kansai, Japan	3.2

Source: United States Department of Transportation, 2001

New York City

POPULATION

In terms of population, the United States of America is the third-largest country in the world, following China and India. Close to 5 percent of the world's population resides in the United States. The population of the United States has grown steadily from 4 million people in 1790, to 63 million in 1890, to 287 million in 2002. Although it is a highly industrialized nation, the United States has a relatively low population density at 75 people per square mile. About 92 percent of the country's residents were born in the United States.

Ten Most Populated States

State	Population (millions)
1	California	33.9
2	Texas	20.9
3	New York	19.0
4	Florida	16.0
5	Illinois	12.4
6	Pennsylvania	12.3
7	Ohio	11.4
8	Michigan	10.0
9	New Jersey	8.4
10	Georgia	8.2

Source: United States Census, 2000

Ten Most Densely Populated States

State	People/Sq. Mile
1	New Jersey	1,094
2	Rhode Island	946
3	Massachusetts	784
4	Connecticut	676
5	Maryland	525
6	New York	385
7	Delaware	380
8	Florida	276
9	Ohio	274
10	Pennsylvania	268

Source: United States Census, 2000

▓▓▓ **More than 12 million immigrants entered the United States through the Ellis Island immigration center in New York City. It closed in 1954.**

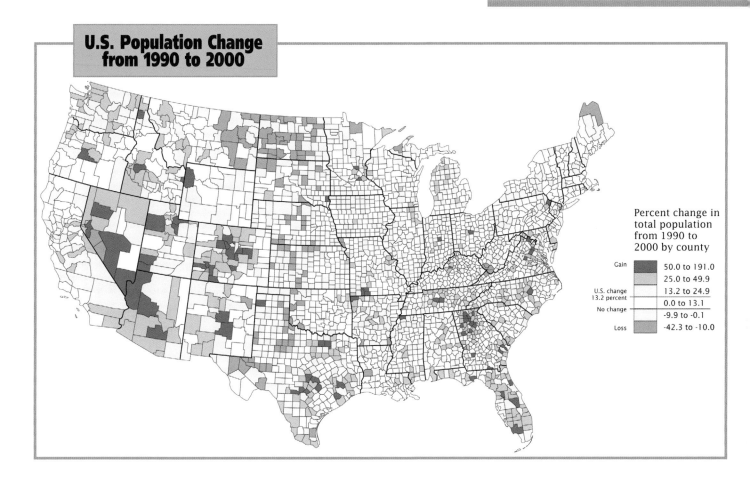

U.S. Population Change from 1990 to 2000

Percent change in total population from 1990 to 2000 by county

Gain	50.0 to 191.0
	25.0 to 49.9
U.S. change 13.2 percent	13.2 to 24.9
	0.0 to 13.1
No change	-9.9 to -0.1
Loss	-42.3 to -10.0

United States Population by Decade from 1900 to 2000

Decade	Population (millions)
1900	76.0
1910	92.0
1920	105.7
1930	122.8
1940	131.7
1950	151.0
1960	179.3
1970	203.3
1980	226.5
1990	248.7
2000	281.4

Source: United States Census, 2000

Ten Most Populated Cities in the United States

City		Population (millions)
1	New York, NY	8.0
2	Los Angeles, CA	3.7
3	Chicago, IL	2.9
4	Houston, TX	2.0
5	Philadelphia, PA	1.5
6	Phoenix, AZ	1.3
7	San Diego, CA	1.2
=	Dallas, TX	1.2
9	San Antonio, TX	1.1
10	Detroit, MI	1.0

Source: United States Census, 2000

CULTURAL GROUPS

In terms of ancestry, the United States has one of the world's most mixed populations. This means that the country's residents are descended from people all over the world. The first people to inhabit what is now the United States were Native Americans. People from Europe, most notably Spain, began to settle the area in the 1500s. Settlers from England and France quickly followed. Soon, large numbers of immigrants from northern and western Europe flocked to America. By the mid-1800s, the largest groups making the journey included people from Denmark, Germany, Ireland, the Netherlands, Norway, Scotland, and Sweden. These groups were soon followed by people from southern and eastern European nations, such as Austria-Hungary, Greece, and Russia.

Top Ten Languages Spoken at Home in the United States

	Language	Speakers (millions)
1	English (only)	198.6
2	Spanish	17.3
3	French	1.7
4	German	1.5
5	Italian	1.3
6	Chinese	1.2
7	Tagalog	0.8
8	Polish	0.7
9	Korean	0.6
10	Vietnamese	0.5

Source: United States Census, Population Division, 1990

Immigration to the U.S. from 1901 to 1998

Period	Immigrants (millions)
1901–1910	8.8
1911–1920	5.7
1921–1930	4.1
1931–1940	0.5
1941–1950	1.0
1951–1960	2.5
1961–1970	3.3
1971–1980	4.5
1981–1990	7.3
1991–1998	7.6

Source: United States Census, 1999

Most Hispanic Americans living in the United States today immigrated from Latin America, or are descendants of immigrants from Latin America. A small percentage of the Hispanic-American population can trace their ancestry directly back to Spain.

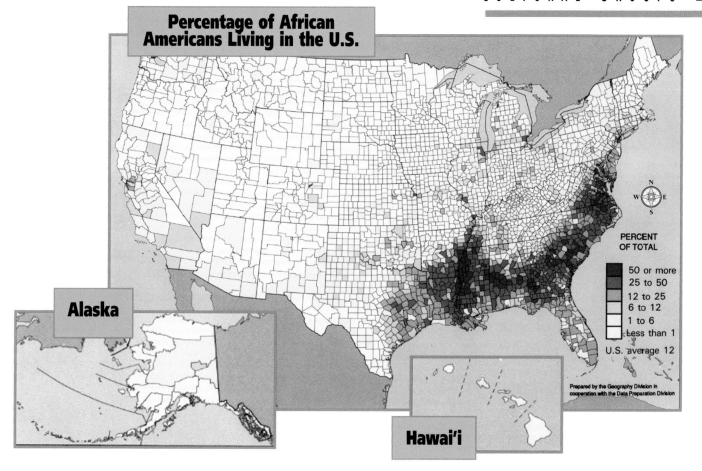

Percentage of African Americans Living in the U.S.

Alaska

Hawai'i

PERCENT OF TOTAL

50 or more
25 to 50
12 to 25
6 to 12
1 to 6
Less than 1

U.S. average 12

Prepared by the Geography Division in cooperation with the Data Preparation Division

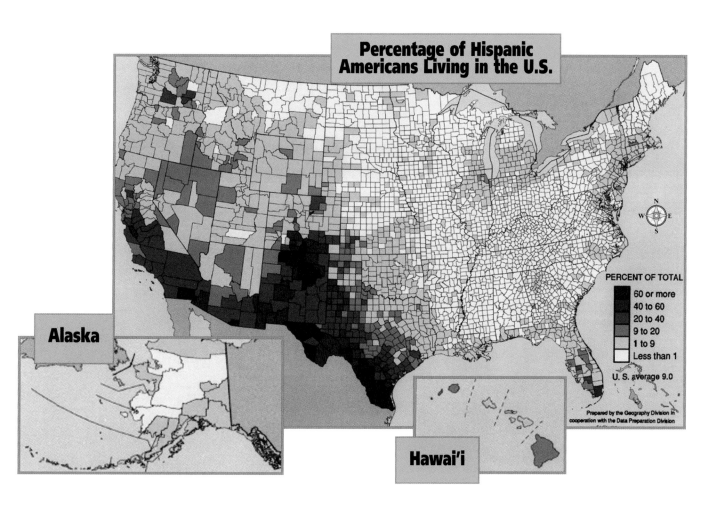

Percentage of Hispanic Americans Living in the U.S.

Alaska

Hawai'i

PERCENT OF TOTAL

60 or more
40 to 60
20 to 40
9 to 20
1 to 9
Less than 1

U. S. average 9.0

Prepared by the Geography Division in cooperation with the Data Preparation Division

NATIVE AMERICANS

When the first European settlers arrived in the 1500s, the Native Americans inhabiting the land were made up of diverse groups with distinct cultures. Native Americans lived in the north, east, south, and west, and had strong ties to the land. Many groups provided for themselves through hunting, fishing, or farming. The arrival of people from Europe to North America threatened the cultures, and the very livelihoods, of the Native Americans. Instead of losing their culture, they fought to protect their way of life and their legal rights. Today, Native Americans, many of whom are living on reservations, continue to embrace and uphold their traditional way of life.

Top Ten Native-American Groups in the United States

Group		Population
1	Cherokee	369,035
2	Navajo	225,298
3	Chippewa	105,988
4	Sioux	107,321
5	Choctaw	86,231
6	Pueblo	55,330
7	Apache	53,330
8	Iroquois	52,557
9	Lumbee	50,888
10	Creek	45,872

Source: United States Census, 1990

Top Ten Native-American Languages Spoken at Home*

Language		Speakers
1	Athapascan-Eyak	157,694
2	Uto-Aztecan	23,493
3	Siouan	19,683
4	Muskogean	13,772
5	Algonquian	12,887
6	Iroquoian	12,046
7	Keres	8,346
8	Tanoan	8,255
9	Penutian	8,190
10	Hokan	2,430

Source: U.S. Bureau of the Census, 1990

*Excluding unspecified Native American languages

▇▇ Powwows and festivals, such as the Red Earth Festival in Oklahoma City, are held across the United States to celebrate Native-American culture.

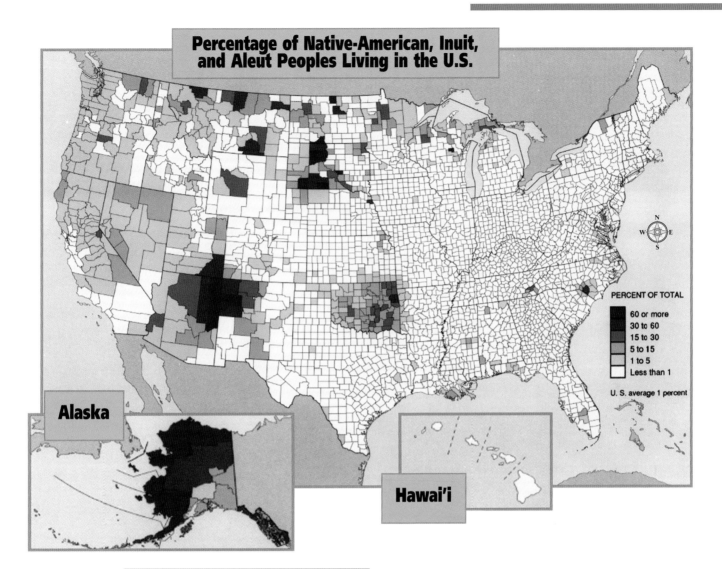

Percentage of Native-American, Inuit, and Aleut Peoples Living in the U.S.

Alaska

Hawai'i

PERCENT OF TOTAL

- 60 or more
- 30 to 60
- 15 to 30
- 5 to 15
- 1 to 5
- Less than 1

U. S. average 1 percent

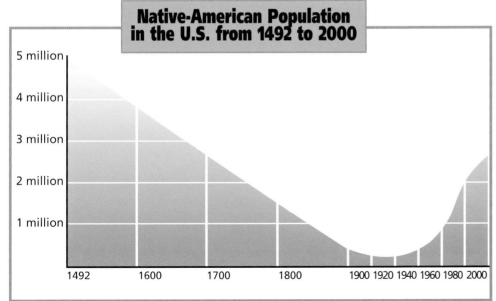

Native-American Population in the U.S. from 1492 to 2000

5 million
4 million
3 million
2 million
1 million

1492   1600   1700   1800   1900 1920 1940 1960 1980 2000

The chart above shows the dramatic decrease in the Native-American population after Europeans came to North America.

States with the Largest Native American Populations*

State	Population
1 California	333,346
2 Oklahoma	273,230
3 Arizona	255,879
4 New Mexico	173,483
5 Texas	118,362
6 North Carolina	99,551
7 Alaska	98,043
8 Washington	93,301
9 New York	82,461
10 South Dakota	62,283

Source: United States Census 2000

*Includes Native-American and Alaska Native populations

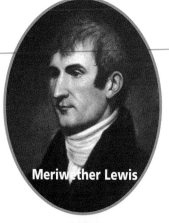

Meriwether Lewis

William Clark

A NATION IS BORN

Brave and adventurous people from many parts of the world helped form the United States. Lured by the fur trade and the wealth of natural resources, explorers came to North America in the 1500s and 1600s. Colonists, mostly British, soon followed. Many settled along the eastern coast of North America. These colonists, living under British rule, created a series of thriving settlements. They declared independence and formed the United States of America in 1776.

As the population grew, Americans spread out across North America. Wherever they went, settlers worked hard to create a new life. They cut down forests and plowed stretches of prairie for farmland. Others mined natural resources, such as gold and silver, and established towns where these minerals were found. Cities were founded along the main transportation routes. Quickly, the country's rapid economic growth turned the United States into a land of great wealth.

Lewis and Clark made the first overland exploration of the American West.

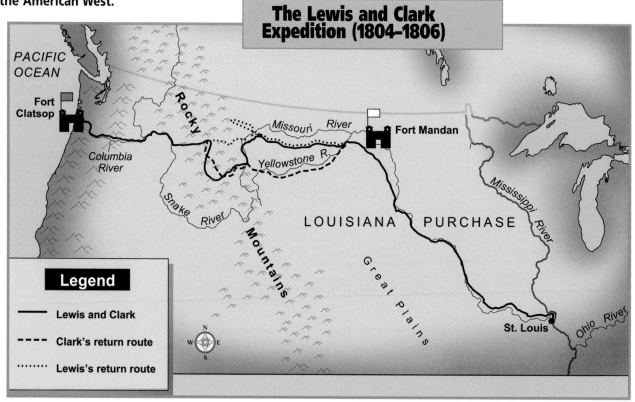

The Lewis and Clark Expedition (1804–1806)

PACIFIC OCEAN

Fort Clatsop

Columbia River

Rocky

Snake River

Mountains

Missouri River

Yellowstone R.

Fort Mandan

LOUISIANA PURCHASE

Great Plains

Mississippi River

St. Louis

Ohio River

Legend

— Lewis and Clark

--- Clark's return route

······ Lewis's return route

Original Thirteen States in the United States

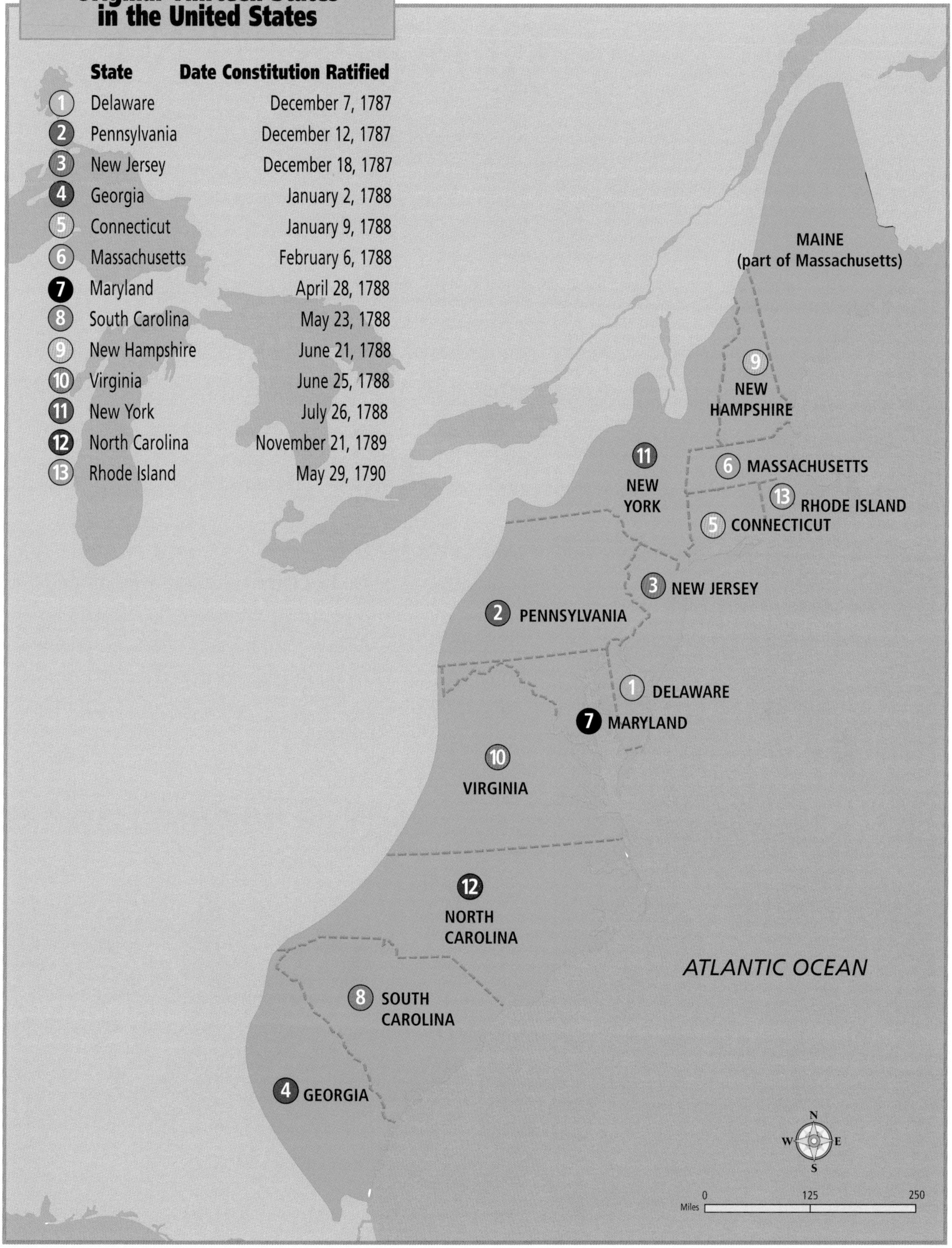

	State	Date Constitution Ratified
1	Delaware	December 7, 1787
2	Pennsylvania	December 12, 1787
3	New Jersey	December 18, 1787
4	Georgia	January 2, 1788
5	Connecticut	January 9, 1788
6	Massachusetts	February 6, 1788
7	Maryland	April 28, 1788
8	South Carolina	May 23, 1788
9	New Hampshire	June 21, 1788
10	Virginia	June 25, 1788
11	New York	July 26, 1788
12	North Carolina	November 21, 1789
13	Rhode Island	May 29, 1790

MAINE
(part of Massachusetts)

9 NEW HAMPSHIRE

11 NEW YORK

6 MASSACHUSETTS

13 RHODE ISLAND

5 CONNECTICUT

3 NEW JERSEY

2 PENNSYLVANIA

1 DELAWARE

7 MARYLAND

10 VIRGINIA

12 NORTH CAROLINA

ATLANTIC OCEAN

8 SOUTH CAROLINA

4 GEORGIA

N
W E
S

0   125   250
Miles

GOVERNMENT

The government of the United States is composed of federal, state, and local divisions. The federal government is based in Washington, DC, which is also home to the White House. The Constitution of the United States provides the legal basis of the government. Drawn up in 1787, the constitution was created to protect the rights of America's citizens.

The United States government is composed of three branches: legislative, judicial, and executive. The legislative branch of government consists of Congress and its two chambers, the Senate and the House of Representatives. The House of Representatives, based on state populations, has 435 seats. The Senate has 100 seats. The judicial branch of government interprets federal law. It consists of the Supreme Court and the lower federal courts. The power of the executive branch is vested in the President of the United States.

Presidents of the United States	
1789–1797	George Washington
1797–1801	John Adams
1801–1809	Thomas Jefferson
1809–1817	James Madison
1817–1825	James Monroe
1825–1829	John Quincy Adams
1829–1837	Andrew Jackson
1837–1841	Martin Van Buren
1841	William Henry Harrison
1841–1845	John Tyler
1845–1849	James K. Polk
1849–1850	Zachary Taylor
1850–1853	Millard Fillmore
1853–1857	Franklin Pierce
1857–1861	James Buchanan
1861–1865	Abraham Lincoln
1865–1869	Andrew Johnson
1869–1877	Ulysses S. Grant
1877–1881	Rutherford Birchard Hayes
1881–1885	Chester Alan Arthur
1885–1889	Stephen Grover Cleveland
1889–1893	Benjamin Harrison
1893–1897	Grover Cleveland
1897–1901	William McKinley
1901–1909	Theodore Roosevelt
1909–1913	William Howard Taft
1913–1921	Thomas Woodrow Wilson
1921–1923	Warren Gamaliel Harding
1923–1929	John Calvin Coolridge
1929–1933	Herbert Clark Hoover
1933–1945	Franklin Delano Roosevelt
1945–1953	Harry S. Truman
1953–1961	Dwight David Eisenhower
1961–1963	John Fitzgerald Kennedy
1963–1969	Lyndon Baines Johnson
1969–1974	Richard Milhous Nixon
1974–1977	Gerald Rudolph Ford
1977–1981	James Earl Carter
1981–1989	Ronald Wilson Reagan
1989–1993	George Herbert Walker Bush
1993–2001	William Jefferson Clinton
2001–	George Walker Bush

George Washington, pictured here on the state seal of Washington, was elected the first president of the United States on February 4, 1789.

The Three Branches of Government

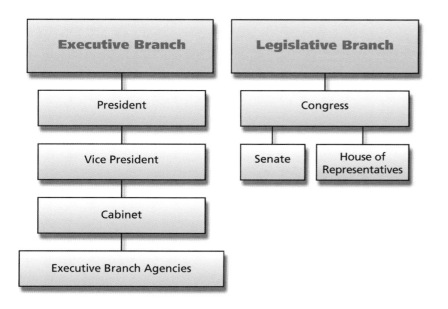

Executive Branch
- President
- Vice President
- Cabinet
- Executive Branch Agencies

Legislative Branch
- Congress
  - Senate
  - House of Representatives

Judicial Branch
- Supreme Court
- Courts of Appeal
- District Courts
- Other Specialized Courts

■■■ The Capitol of the United States serves as the seat of the U.S. Congress. This building sits on Capitol Hill in Washington, DC.

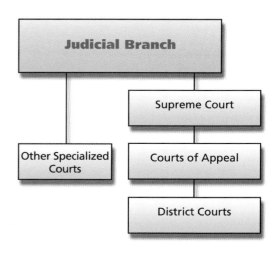

Ten Youngest U.S. Presidents

	President	Age at Presidency
1	Theodore Roosevelt	42
2	John F. Kennedy	43
3	William Jefferson Clinton	46
=	Ulysses S. Grant	46
5	Grover Cleveland	47
6	Franklin Pierce	48
7	James A. Garfield	49
=	James K. Polk	49
9	Millard Fillmore	50
=	Chester Alan Arthur	50

Source: www.whitehouse.gov

State Statistics

State Name	State Abbreviation	Area of State (square miles)	Population (Census 2000)	Population Density	Joined Union
Alabama	AL	52,237	4,447,100	85	December 14, 1819
Alaska	AK	615,230	626,932	1	January 3, 1959
Arizona	AZ	114,006	5,130,632	45	February 14, 1912
Arkansas	AR	53,182	2,673,400	50	June 15, 1836
California	CA	158,869	33,871,648	213	September 9, 1850
Colorado	CO	104,100	4,301,261	41	August 1, 1876
Connecticut	CT	5,544	3,405,565	614	January 9, 1788
Delaware	DE	2,396	83,600	35	December 7, 1787
Florida	FL	59,928	15,982,378	267	March 3, 1845
Georgia	GA	58,977	8,186,453	139	January 2, 1788
Hawai'i	HI	6,459	1,211,537	188	August 21, 1959
Idaho	ID	83,574	1,293,953	15	July 3, 1890
Illinois	IL	57,918	12,419,293	214	December 3, 1818
Indiana	IN	36,420	6,080,485	167	December 11, 1816
Iowa	IA	56,276	2,926,324	52	December 28, 1846
Kansas	KS	82,282	2,688,418	33	January 29, 1861
Kentucky	KY	40,411	4,041,769	100	June 1, 1792
Louisiana	LA	49,651	4,468,976	90	April 30, 1812
Maine	ME	33,741	1,274,923	38	March 15, 1820
Maryland	MD	12,297	5,296,486	431	April 28, 1788
Massachusetts	MA	9,241	6,349,097	687	February 6, 1788
Michigan	MI	96,705	9,938,444	103	January 26, 1837
Minnesota	MN	86,943	4,919,479	57	May 11, 1858
Mississippi	MS	48,286	2,844,658	59	December 10, 1817
Missouri	MO	69,709	5,595,211	80	August 10, 1821

State Name	State Abbreviation	Area of State (square miles)	Population (Census 2000)	Population Density	Joined Union
Montana	MT	147,046	902,195	6	November 8, 1889
Nebraska	NE	77,358	1,711,263	22	March 1, 1867
Nevada	NV	110,567	1,998,257	18	October 31, 1864
New Hampshire	NH	9,283	1,235,786	133	June 21, 1788
New Jersey	NJ	8,215	8,414,350	1,024	December 18, 1787
New Mexico	NM	121,598	1,819,046	15	January 6, 1912
New York	NY	53,989	18,976,457	351	July 26, 1788
North Carolina	NC	52,672	8,049,313	153	November 21, 1789
North Dakota	ND	70,704	642,200	9	November 2, 1889
Ohio	OH	44,828	11,353,140	253	March 1, 1803
Oklahoma	OK	69,903	3,450,654	49	November 16, 1907
Oregon	OR	97,132	3,421,399	35	February 14, 1859
Pennsylvania	PA	46,058	12,281,054	267	December 12, 1787
Rhode Island	RI	1,231	1,048,319	852	May 29, 1790
South Carolina	SC	31,189	4,012,012	129	May 23, 1788
South Dakota	SD	77,121	2,688,418	35	November 2, 1889
Tennessee	TN	42,146	4,041,769	96	June 1, 1796
Texas	TX	267,277	20,851,820	78	December 29, 1845
Utah	UT	84,904	2,233,169	26	January 4, 1896
Vermont	VT	9,615	608,827	63	March 4, 1791
Virginia	VA	42,326	7,078,515	167	June 25, 1788
Washington	WA	70,637	5,894,121	83	November 11, 1889
West Virginia	WV	24,231	1,808,344	75	June 20, 1863
Wisconsin	WI	65,499	5,363,675	82	May 29, 1848
Wyoming	WY	97,818	493,782	5	July 10, 1890

WEB SITES

50 States

www.50states.com

This great Web site provides a wealth of information on important state statistics and symbols. It profiles state symbols such as birds, songs, and flags. Visitors to this Web site can also find sports, tourism, and population information for any of the fifty states.

Geobop's North America

www.geobop.com/World/NA

The Geobop Web site provides quick facts, symbols, geography, and historical and statistical information for every state in the country. This is a great site for research projects.

U.S. Census Bureau

www.census.gov

Surf over to this Web site to find official census information, statistical profiles, and projections for just about every topic of national importance. Visitors can find population statistics, economic profiles, and housing information for the United States.

National Park Guide

www.nps.gov/parks.html

This Web site lists and profiles every national park in the United States. If you are thinking about visiting Yellowstone National Park, or any other national park in the U.S., this is the site for you. Additional information is provided through photographs, maps, and key dates.

INDEX